This book is dedicated to my wife, Randi.

You have listened to every one of my crazy ideas.
You have been through every up and down
I have ever experienced in business.
You have been there for me when I'm doing great and
you have been there for me when I haven't been.
I owe the life I currently have to you.
Everything I am, everything I have and
everything I do could not have been possible
if I didn't have you by my side.
Thank you for keeping your faith in me and
thank you for everything you do for me.
I love you more than you will ever know.

Many Thanks

Cindy Anderson—You approached me two years ago and said you could help my business. I am SO glad I took you up on your offer. You pushed me, you challenged me and you made me look at my speaking as a real business. Your help and advice with this book were invaluable. I would not be where I am today if it wasn't for you. You will never have any idea how grateful I am to you.

Ed Scannell—You met with me before I ever knew what I wanted to speak about and you gave me of your time and your advice. Every time I had a question, you were always there with the right answer. You have made my journey of becoming a professional speaker much smoother. I'm proud to call you my mentor.

Vic O'Steen—You spoke at our May 2003 NSA meeting and you said that writing a book is a great way to build your speaking business. After seeing the books that you and Larry Winget wrote, I knew I could do it. I left that meeting on May 10, 2003, started my book that afternoon and finished the first draft one week later. Thanks for whatever you said that made so much sense to me.

Paula Wigboldy—If I didn't have you with me, this book would have taken another year or more to finish. Knowing that I have someone like you in my corner, following up on every call, every lead, and every contact, allowed me the time to make this dream of writing a book a reality. Thank you for all you do for me. You are the VERY best!

Allan Starr—Every time I needed sound advice about so many things with this book, you were always there to lend a helping hand. In fact, without your help, I never would have come up with the right title for my book. Thanks for everything you've done and for everything you'll do in the future

Contents

Introduction

Hi. My name is Dave Sherman and I am The Networking Guy™. Thanks for taking a look at my book. I am assuming that you might be standing in a book store right now or at one of my many presentations, deciding whether you should invest some of your hard-earned cash in my book. If you want my opinion, I say, "Go for it!" My wife and my kids would really appreciate it.

However, if you need a bit more assistance in making your decision, allow me to help.

You might be asking "How will networking benefit me?" Here are a few ways:

- You will be able to do more in less time, with less aggravation, and with better results. How is this possible? By networking, so you don't have to do everything by yourself. By creating and nurturing a powerful network of people you know and trust, you can rely upon them to help you do the things you might not be great at doing yourself. Your network can help you become better at everything you do.

- Your whole life will become a bit simpler than before. Why? As I just mentioned, you will now know great people you can call at a moment's notice to ask for advice, suggestions, assistance, or just to talk. When you realize that you no longer have to have all the answers, it takes a tremendous weight off your shoulders.

- You will start impacting people's lives at a very deep level. I'm getting ahead of myself but my definition of networking is to be a personal and professional resource for others and *expect nothing in return*! When you start to help people without any expectation of getting something in return, you will experience fulfillment like you have never felt before and people will start feeling much more connected to you than ever before.

As you can see, networking will help in all areas of your life. It's not just for business anymore. Besides growing my business, I have found jobs for myself and others, I have found people to help take care of my kids while my wife and I were out of the country, and I even used networking to help me come up with the title and cover art for this book. I am the person I am today because of the networking I have done over the past 20 years.

Another question you might be asking yourself is "Why is now such a good time to start networking?" Allow me to provide a few reasons why you need networking more today than ever before:

- There are more home-based businesses in the United States than ever before. While it's great to be able to work in your pajamas, most people find the biggest challenge to working at home is not having anyone to talk to. By establishing a solid network, they can always have the right people to reach out to at any moment. Plus, by finding the right place to network, they will always have lots of people to mingle and schmooze with.

- If you have been through a round or two of layoffs in your company and you still have your job, the depth of your network might have had a lot to do with you keeping your job. When it comes to laying off people in any company, management will always keep the ones who are connected the best and know the most people. If you spend time getting to know the other people in your company, your job security will skyrocket!

- You might think that you don't need to spend much time networking because you have everything you need right now. However, networking doesn't help you with what you need today. It helps with all the things that you don't know you're going to need tomorrow. You've heard the old saying, "Today is the first day of the rest of your life." Well, today is the day that you can start to build a powerful network that will help you for the rest of your life. Tomorrow might be another day but wouldn't it be great if you knew you had the people in place to help you with just about anything you need.

The last question you might have for me concerns the reputation that networking currently holds in the United States. Here is the most important thing for you to understand: What most people today see as networking really isn't networking at all. What is it? It's called "prospecting." Prospecting is the process of finding people who you can sell your product or service to. That's not networking. Networking is helping *other* people sell *their* products or services. It's helping *other* people achieve *their* goals and desires. This book shows you step by step how to start helping others get what they want and, in return, you will begin to see people helping you get what you want.

Another area that confuses people is how networking is different than network marketing. Network marketing is a business structure in which a distributor network is needed to build the business. Usually such businesses are also multi-level, which means that participants get payouts for networks they establish. While there are many honest and very profitable network marketing organizations, many of them are nothing more than pyramid schemes, get-rich-quick programs or worse. Bottom line, networking is something that will help you grow your business, get ahead at your current job, and make almost every area of your life simpler.

Albert Einstein said, "The definition of insanity is doing the same thing over and over again and expecting a different result." With this in mind, you now have two choices. You can put this book back down on the shelf or table and continue to do things the way you always have and pray for a different result, or you can take this book up to the cashier or maybe bring it directly to me (I'd be glad to sign it for you) and begin to stop the insanity and start using networking to help others and have them help you too. If you find you have other questions regarding my book, please feel free to call me at 480-860-6100. I hope you decide to purchase my book. I promise it will start making your business and your life better the day you start using it.

Action Plan Instructions

You will notice that at the end of many of the tips there is a box titled "Action Plan." These boxes are meant to encourage you to select a specific date that you will start using one of my 50 tips. After reading each tip, if you feel that you would like to apply that tip to your everyday life, select a date or a goal. Also, make sure you fold down the corner of the page so you know where to find each of the tips you want to start using.

When you meet your goal, unfold the page and go on to the next one. When you have unfolded every page, you will be a powerful networking professional, networking more effectively, more comfortably, and more profitably.

Basic
Networking

1 Give first and expect nothing in return.

Q. I've been in sales for years and I consider myself pretty good at networking. However, you say that what I'm doing isn't networking. What is your definition of networking?

Dave: What is your definition of networking? Over the years, I have asked hundreds of people this question and am always amazed at the variety of answers I receive. Here are a few:

- "Meeting as many people as I can."
- "Finding people who can help me get what I need."
- "Talking to people about my product."
- "Getting business cards from as many people as possible."

As you can see, there are many answers to this simple question. My definition of networking is: Being a valuable business and personal resource, such as doing what you can to help other people reach their goals and desires, and expecting nothing in return. Expecting nothing in return usually catches people off guard, considering everyone wants to get something when they network.

Zig Ziglar, one of the greatest motivational speakers of our time says, "If you help enough people get what they want, they will help you get what you want." It must, however, be done in this order. You cannot approach networking as, "I'll help you or give you some business after you have helped me." You must be pro-active and help other people first!

Let me share an example. As a professional speaker, I travel a lot and spend many nights in hotels. No matter which hotel chain I am staying with, there is always a Bible in the room. I must confess I haven't read much of the Bible, but I know it says something like, "He who gives shall receive." It doesn't say, "He who has received a lot should give back too." I believe, if it's good for the big guy upstairs, it should be good for you too.

✔ **Action Plan:**

I will share this concept of networking with three or more people by _____.

Network, don't prospect.

Q. If most people aren't networking when they think they are, what are they doing?

Dave: Think back to the last networking function you attended. How many of the people you met handed you their business cards whether you wanted them or not? How many spent what must have felt like a huge amount of time telling you everything you never wanted to know about their products or services? What was your reaction to these people? Did you have a strong desire to do business with them, or did you just want to get away?

What these people were doing was prospecting. They were on the prowl to make a sale. You know the people I'm talking about. They launch into their sales pitches before they know anything about you. They also immediately lose interest if they find out you don't have any interest in their products or services.

There is nothing wrong with prospecting. It is something every businessperson needs to do. However, there is a big difference between networking and prospecting. Once you understand this difference, you will never approach a networking function in the same way again.

> ✔ **Action Plan:**
> I will reread the first two tips in this book at least two more times by _____.

Give the most to receive the most.

*Q. Then, if I understand you correctly, networking is
   about give and take, right?*

Dave: You are half right. Networking is about giving. It's
that simple. You give, and you give, and you keep giving!
The people who give the most will receive the most. If you
take the time to find out what other people need and you
help them get it, they will be forever connected to you.

This concept really comes into play if you are slightly
timid. Imagine how comfortable networking would be if
all you did were to help other people achieve their goals
and desires. Just think about it. The next time you walk
into a networking function, you can look across the room
and ask yourself, "Who can I help today?," instead of
"Who can I sell to today?"

✔ **Action Plan:**

Beginning on _____, I will seek out people
who I can help instead of only trying to sell to them.

Give, even to the takers.

Q. How do you deal with people who only take, and take, and take?

Dave: Keep giving to them. I know, I know. That's probably not what you were expecting to hear.

Close your eyes for a minute and think of someone who always wants something from you. Someone who always asks for favors or business leads, or for things you aren't really comfortable providing. It would be much easier to blow that person off and never speak to him or her again. Yet, no one ever said that the person you help would be the one who helps you, only that if you give, you shall receive.

I know a gentleman who is the vice president of a very large bank. He told me he would go crazy trying to reciprocate to everyone who helps him. I helped him to understand that true networking is an on-going cycle, not tit for tat. When he gives of himself, he will start to receive, many times from those for whom he has done nothing.

✔ Action Plan:

By _____, I will do something to help people I know even if they can't do anything that will directly help me.

---

5 **Create a network that supports you.**

Q. People I talk to say that to grow my business, I have to get out there and network. Why?

Dave: Have you heard of the Lone Ranger? The big cowboy with the black mask and the white horse? Do you know why he was called the Lone Ranger? Probably because he always wanted to do everything by himself. But even the Lone Ranger needed help now and then. So, he had his trusty sidekick, Tonto.

Do you try to do everything yourself, like the Lone Ranger, because you feel that's the way it should be done? Donna Fisher, author of *Power Networking*, calls this the Lone Ranger Syndrome.

Wouldn't it be great if you had a trusty sidekick to help you when you needed it? With a strong network, you do. Your network is your trusty sidekick. Consider this:

- When you have people you can depend on, you can get more done in less time because you don't have to do everything yourself.

   Can you personally do everything that needs to be done for your job or business? If so, you're probably the only person on earth who can. I know I can't. I have a technical person who keeps my Web site looking and performing great. I have a marketing person who follows up with almost every person I meet. I have support people who take care of all the little things I never have time to do. My network is very important to me because it provides me with the strength of a group.

■ Networking helps you keep an eye on your competition, because you have so many more eyes looking out for you.

In this very competitive business environment, it's vitally important to keep an eye on your competition. It doesn't matter whether you are an employee monitoring who's in line for that next great promotion, or a business owner watching out for new companies breaking into your market. With a powerful network in place, you will always know what's happening in your industry.

For example, a friend of mine once learned a co-worker was intentionally harming her reputation because he wanted her position. She found this out from someone in her network and was able to address the issue and save her job.

This is especially important if you own your business. Alone, you don't have the resources to keep an eye out for potential threats to your business. By building up your network of contacts and communicating with them on a regular basis, you'll always have someone watching your back while you are focused on the bottom line.

■ When you have a strong network of people you trust and respect, you have the support to try new ideas, products and concepts.

If you had a new idea for your job or business, would you implement it immediately? No way! You would probably ask people for their advice and opinions to decide whether to move ahead, make changes, or scrap the idea. With a network, you have the freedom to come up with the most creative and original ideas because you can depend on others to help you make the best possible decisions. My network made this book possible. I turned to them with dozens of questions and they always delivered. The title for this book was created from ideas I received from my network.

- Creating a worldwide network provides you with much more information than you can get in your own hometown.

With the invention of fax machines, cell phones, and e-mail, the world has become a much smaller place. You can now build strong contacts around the world, expanding your network. This applies equally to business owners and employees.

A good friend of mine in Phoenix works for a charity raising money for people in need. Through his network of contacts around the United States, he learned about a campaign tool a Minneapolis charity used to raise significantly more money than before. He applied this new tool to his campaign and he too raised more money than ever before.

- A strong network provides greater job security.

With a downturn in the economy, companies lay off large portions of their staffs. How can you lessen your chances of being let go? Work at building your network. If you are an employee, this is probably the best reason to develop a strong network of people. If you are the person your company turns to for information about a wide range of topics, you are much more valuable. This is a perfect example of the adage, "It's not what you know, it's who you know."

If you are laid off, having an extensive network of people to turn to is one of your most important assets.

Networking is for everyone. It's there to provide support when you need it.

✔ **Action Plan:**

I will share this great idea with a friend by
_____.

Address specific people needs through your network.

Q. I have a typical "Type A" personality. I want success and I want it NOW. I don't like wasting time so I cut to the chase. Are there specific people I need to network with?

Dave: Yes, but the first thing I will tell you is slow down and relax! You and I have a lot in common. I too, have a Type A personality. On top of that, I have mainstream Attention Deficit Disorder, which is a biologically based condition causing a persistent pattern of difficulties resulting in one or more of the following behaviors: inattention, hyperactivity, and impulsivity. Because of this, instant gratification is not fast enough, so I completely understand where you're coming from.

To answer your question, there are specific people you want to network with, and you determine who these specific people are. But first, you need a plan.

Start by making a list of the people and industries you'd like to know better, or with whom you'd like to create deeper connections or do more business. Just let your mind wander and jot down every person or industry you think of. As you are doing this, always remember my definition of networking (being a valuable business and personal resource for others and expecting nothing in return). These are people you can help to achieve their goals and desires, not just sell a product or service. Financial planners, the chairperson of your country club, even the left-handed, red-haired, Spanish-speaking piano teachers—

write them all down. That last one might be hard to find, but with a little work, you can connect with just about anyone.

Once you've finished your list, ask people you know who are in the same industries or networking circles where to find these people. If you talk to enough people, you can learn where financial planners network, where your country club chair mingles, and where that oh-so-elusive left-handed, red-haired, Spanish-speaking piano teacher socializes as well.

✔ **Action Plan:**

By _____, I will create a list of people I would like to have in my network.

Cover all the bases when creating your network.

Q. I am developing a nice network of people, however there isn't much variety in the professions or businesses they represent. Are there specific lines of work my network should have covered?

Dave: Yes. The three most important people in your network are your doctor, your accountant, and your attorney. These people will make sure you are always healthy, wealthy, and wise.

In addition, one of the greatest networkers in the world, Harvey Mackay, says there are 16 people every network should have, especially because of their value in an emergency. Harvey MacKay is the author of *Swim with the Sharks Without Being Eaten*, *Beware the Naked Man Who Offers You His Shirt*, and *Dig Your Well Before You're Thirsty*. Like me, you probably don't have all of these yet.

- Real estate broker, for the latest developments in real estate

- Ticket broker, for those impossible-to-find tickets for that great client

- Travel agent, to come to your rescue when your flight's been canceled and you're stuck in some tiny airport

- Religious leader, for a little faith

- Headhunter, for those times you need one

- Banker, to help keep an eye on your money

- Elected local official, because it's always nice to have powerful friends in high places

- High-ranking police officer, when you need to get out of a ticket

- Firefighter, because there's no better person to know in any kind of emergency

- Celebrity, when a little name dropping is needed

- Veterinarian, so your pet gets the best and brightest vet on earth

- Insurance agent, because you might never talk to your agent, but when you need him, you need him now!

- Divorce lawyer, just in case you need to get out of a bad situation

- Auto mechanic, when you need a new gizmo for your doohickey and want to buy it from someone you really trust

- Media contact, so you can see your name in print more often

- Best friend, no explanation needed.

There could be others. Whatever the case, the time to start looking for them is long before you ever need them.

✔ **Action Plan:**

Starting _____, I will seek out as many of the 16 types of people on the above list as I can.

Select the best networking groups for you.

Q. As someone who's new to networking, I'd like to know where is the very best place to network?

Dave: This is one of the most frequently asked questions. My answer is simple, yet complicated. I know. That's an oxymoron, like jumbo shrimp, small crowd, legally drunk, or 12-ounce pound cake.

My simple-yet-complicated answer is, there is no best place for people to network. What works for me might not work for you.

As a professional speaker, I have great networking opportunities with the National Speakers Association. However, unless you speak as part of your business, this group wouldn't work well for you. You need to find an organization that fits you and do your best to network within that group.

If you're not sure where to start, pick a group that looks good and go! Every group I have known will allow you to attend as a guest, sometimes multiple times before asking you to pay dues. Once there, you can determine if the group fits your needs. If it does, look into becoming a member. If not, thank them for letting you check it out and move on.

Many people try to predict whether or not a group will work for them before they even walk through the door. Can't be done. The only way to find out is to get off your butt and check it out! There are thousands of networking groups. Pick one, give it a try, and see what happens. You might be pleasantly surprised.

✔ Action Plan:

Within the next month, I will select three to five networking groups to attend as a guest to see if they fit my networking needs.

9

Look to newspapers, chambers of commerce, and people you know for the best networking groups for you.

Q. I have just opened my own business. When I talk to people about the best way to get the word out, everyone mentions networking. Where can I find a list of networking groups?

Dave: Here are several sources to help you find groups that would work for you, regardless of whether you have just started your business, have an established business, or want to move up in your current job:

- The local daily newspaper. Check out the business section first. Most groups are listed here.

- The local business newspaper. I live in Phoenix and we have a couple of them. My favorite is *The Business Journal*. If you're looking for an Irish group, a women-only group, a group for home-based businesses, or any other type of networking group, this paper is for you. *Business Journals* are distributed in more than 40 cities. Go to www.BizJournals.com to learn if there is a *Business Journal* in your town.

- Call your local chamber of commerce and find out about the networking groups and activities they offer. More than 90 percent of the people who join a chamber do so to network. Chambers are always putting together programs and groups to help small businesses grow. They offer breakfast, lunch and evening programs, and many have groups for specific interests such as high tech, sales, and minority owned businesses. I have been involved with more than a dozen different chambers, and I think they are some of the best places to network.

- Ask people you know for recommendations. Start with people in your office, and in your industry. Brian Tracy, one of the greatest motivational speakers I know, always says, "If you want to be successful, find successful people and do what they do." If you want to network with these successful people, you need to go where they go.

✔Action Plan:

During the next month, I will actively research networking events to attend.

Know the difference between a leads group and a networking group.

Q. I asked a good friend of mine if she knows of any good networking groups I could join. She told me about a few leads groups that have worked out very well for her. What is the difference between a leads group and a networking group?

Dave: The main goal of a leads group is to find business leads for the members of the group. It is very important to get to know as much as possible about the other members' businesses and for other members to know as much as possible about yours. Members put substantial pressure on each other to generate leads for each other. Some groups even charge a small fine if you don't bring in leads.

A leads group traditionally meets at the same time and place on a weekly, bi-weekly, monthly or yearly basis, to encourage relationship-building. Many groups are comprised of one business professional from a chosen field, eliminating the competition for specific business leads. Other groups place restrictions on the length of time you are in business, or the level of responsibility you hold in a firm, when deciding who to accept for membership. Restrictions are placed on group membership to ensure it is composed of business professionals who are looking for the same thing and playing by the same rules. These restrictions also can help eliminate conflicts within a group, allowing for easier relationship-building. Some groups have no restrictions at all.

A networking group is a gathering of business people and other professionals who meet on a regular basis to socialize, make formal presentations on various topics of interest, or chat with one another about their livelihoods.

Networking groups discuss everything from sales leads to marketing and public relations strategies. For the small business owner, the more informal elements of a networking group—the give-and-take of information and guidance among members—can serve as powerful business tools.

Steve Krauser, president of Network Associates, a New York consulting firm that helps networking groups function more efficiently, says, "If nothing else, being out on your own means you lose the subliminal marketing and networking capacity of the corporate machine. A good networking group can address those things."

You'll find a lot less pressure in networking groups. You might want to try to generate leads for members, but it's not a requirement. Networking groups are normally more supportive in nature, and will expose you to more people because they don't limit their membership to one person per industry or profession.

To find out whether you want to join a networking or leads group, try them both. While everyone has an opinion, the only way to decide is to experience both for yourself.

✔ Action Plan:

By _____, I will go see for myself the difference between a networking group and a leads group.

11

Attend breakfast networking groups for the best results.

Q. I have very limited time to network. I know it's something I need to do, but my schedule only will allow me to attend one function per week. I've heard breakfast networking functions are the best. Is this true?

Dave: This is a very tough question to answer. If I say breakfast functions are the best, I'm going to receive nasty e-mails from people who put on lunch and evening functions. Well, The Networking Guy™ doesn't bow down to anyone. In my humble opinion, yes, I think morning events are the best. Here's why:

- One of the toughest issues people deal with at a networking function is creating casual conversation with people they don't know. Because of their structure, which normally is mingling in the beginning of the event, followed by a few announcements, 30-second commercials, testimonials, and a close, morning events make this easy for veterans and rookies alike. People know what they are supposed to do.

- Morning functions provide each person the opportunity to stand in front of the group and give a 30-second commercial. The eyes and ears of everyone in that room are focused on you as you share all of the reasons they should do business with you. (If you're a bit worried about how you build that perfect 30-second commercial, I answer this question later in the book.)

■ Members also share testimonials about the people in the group they have done business with. This is a great way to boast about other members and the great job they did. Just as with networking, before you can begin to receive testimonials, you must first provide excellent service and give testimonials to others.

■ Attending a morning function is a great way to kick off your day. After one or two hours mingling with others, learning how you can help them, you feel great. That feeling sticks with you for hours after the event is over. Plus, most morning functions offer a breakfast buffet, so the breakfast is good. You've heard it all your life—a good breakfast is the best way to start your day.

■ People who drag themselves out of bed that early in the morning are serious about meeting and connecting with others. There is something to be said for people who trade the warmth and comfort of their beds for the opportunity to meet, mingle, and connect with others.

While this is only my opinion, considering I have probably attended more morning networking functions in the past few years than most people will in their entire lives, I would take The Networking Guy's advice, reset your alarm clock, get up early, and see for yourself.

✔ Action Plan:

I will attend a breakfast networking function by

_____.

If you can't get up in the morning, go to evening networking functions.

Q. I'm more of a night owl, not a morning person. What can you tell me about evening networking functions?

Dave: If you hit the snooze button on your alarm clock so many times it no longer works, an evening networking program might be a better alternative for you. Let's explore the pros and cons:

The Pros

- You've just had one of the worst work days of your life. Everything that could go wrong did go wrong, plus a few others things, too. Now that you're done for the day, you can either go work out (yeah right!), go home and try to unwind (that's not always easy), or make a stop at an evening networking function to see a few friends, have some laughs and maybe get a good meal. You might even make a connection for your next big account. Sounds pretty good, doesn't it? It sure as heck sounds a lot better than 30 minutes on the Stairmaster, or some spinning instructor screaming at you to work harder.

- If you feel timid when you network and find it hard to relax, evening programs might work for you because you can get a cocktail to help you feel more comfortable in this environment. Before you blast me for promoting the consumption of alcohol, I am not encouraging people to drink. I am just pointing out a possible option for those who need help to relax.

- Evening functions are more social in nature than a breakfast or lunch event, so they are the perfect place to build stronger relationships with your contacts. After a hard day at work, don't show up and continue talking business. Chat about other things, like your weekend plans, or your favorite hobby. The greatest part about sharing personal information is it gives other people permission to do the same. When you open up about your life, they will normally share something too and that's how connections are deepened.

The Cons

- Evening events traditionally have no structure. When you show up, you check in, walk inside, grab some refreshments, and the rest is up to you. If you want to meet lots of people, it's your responsibility to approach them, introduce yourself, and start up conversations. For many people, this doesn't pose a problem. However, for the majority of people this is a daunting task.

- Because of the social nature of evening functions, people could have different agendas than you. While you might be looking to expand your network, others might be there to find a significant other, or to just hang out and enjoy the free food. With so many possibilities, it's hard to accomplish your goal.

- Anytime alcohol is present at a networking event it completely changes the dynamic of the group. While a cocktail or two might make you more confident and even daring at times, it doesn't allow people to see who you really are. You might not see who others really are either. If you act one way at an event and another at work, this causes confusion in the minds of the people you meet.

I might be a bit biased toward morning networking functions. I attend morning events because I want to be home with my family in the evenings. I made a deal with my wife in 2001. I promised her that unless I was the evening's featured speaker, I would be home with her and my kids. Do I enjoy evening functions? I most certainly do. However, by attending networking functions during other parts of the day, I get to have my networking cake and eat it too.

✔ **Action Plan:**

I will attend an evening networking function by

_____.

Get involved with a charity you care about.

Q. I've been told that giving your time to a worthwhile cause is a great way to meet people. Is volunteering really a great way to connect with people?

Dave: While I've said there is no best place to network, one of the greatest ways to network is by getting involved in a charity or other volunteer organization. Through my involvement in local, regional, and national charitable organizations, I have met some of the best people I know. Plus, getting involved on a national level has expanded my network way beyond my state borders.

You might say to yourself, "I don't have time to give. I barely have enough time to get the things I want to get done now."

I felt the same way. I started getting involved in 1993. I owned a small retail chain and had two small kids at home. I wondered where I would find the time to get involved in something new. You don't find the time, you make the time! We only have 24 hours in a day. Do you make the most effective use of your 24 hours? I didn't. But, all it took was making a few changes and I found the time to help those less fortunate than myself.

✔ Action Plan:

By _____, I will talk to friends and/or family members who are involved with volunteer organizations and I will find out why they enjoy the time they give and how they carve time out of their busy days.

Follow your heart to the right charity for you.

Q. How do you pick an organization?

Dave: You need to follow your heart on this one. You must pick an organization you have the truest and deepest passion for. These are normally organizations that have had some impact on your life, not ones where you think you can meet the richest, most powerful, and most influential people. If you volunteer for a charity to climb the social ladder and don't have true convictions for the group, people will see right through you. You will never be embraced by the powers that be. However, if you believe in the cause, really support the organization, and show them your abilities, skills, and your desire to help, the contacts you can make are limitless.

✔ Action Plan:

By _____, I will make a list of charities and/or volunteer organizations for which I have a TRUE passion. By _____, I will call one of the organizations to see how I can help.

For success, follow the networking experts—women.

Q. For decades, we have compared men and women in every imaginable area. Who is superior in networking?

Dave: Psychologists who have studied networking tell us women are better at it than men. Since they were little girls, women have been taught to share and meet other people's needs. Men do not network as well because it is more difficult to admit they have needs and they have a fear of appearing vulnerable.

Men bond together in ways that make them feel more powerful. One way of achieving that is to exclude people. Historically, men have excluded women from organizations, from the boardroom to the golf course. However, studies have shown that women are learning to network even more effectively with other women. The quality of information, contacts and opportunities they receive as a result is equal to that of male networks.

Now, with the Internet and women's organizations that support advancement, women look to each other for advice, career information, job tips, and employment opportunities. They have created a support system for themselves. These informal strategic alliances can benefit women greatly.

Thank you Advancingwomen.com.

✔**Action Plan:**

By _____, I will ask a successful business-woman how networking has helped her succeed.

16

It's okay to occasionally sell at network-ing events, but don't make it a habit.

Q. *I have heard you speak and you always say that net-working is different from prospecting. However, if my company is running a special on our product or service, I want to make sure people know about it. Is there anything wrong with occasionally going to a networking function with the sole purpose of selling your product or service?*

Dave: Allow me to make a confession. I'm known as The Networking Guy™. I spend a good part of my life helping people embrace the concept that networking is about help-ing others. I must admit, many times over the past ten years I have gone to a networking function to sell my prod-uct or service. I didn't want to help anyone. Oh dear Lord, please forgive me! Okay, I feel much better! I'm glad I got that off my chest. Now, let me continue.

Let's get one thing straight. While networking is the pro-cess of helping others to achieve their goals and desires, the ultimate goal of networking is to grow your business by selling more of your product or service. If you did noth-ing but help others, you would probably have a very fulfilling life, but you would starve!

That said, there is absolutely nothing wrong with occa-sionally attending a networking function to sell your product or service. We all need to sell or we won't be in business very long. I have attended many functions to pro-mote a workshop series, a new book or tape series, or a speaking engagement. My purpose was to find people to purchase tickets or products.

However, remember, if you attend too many functions with the sole purpose of selling your product or service, the connections you have made will begin to suffer. Those people you are trying to connect with will eventually shy away from you because no one likes to be sold all of the time. It's fine occasionally, but don't lose sight of your real goal, which is trying to help *other* people achieve their goals and desires. As long as you keep a good balance between giving and receiving, you can have the very best of both worlds.

✔ **Action Plan:**

I will limit the times that I attend a networking function to primarily sell my product or service starting _____.

The "How to" Guide to Networking Events

Arrive early.

Q. I am not the most punctual person on earth. In fact, I'm seldom on time. Is there anything wrong with arriving fashionably late to a networking event?

Dave: I believe that one of the ways to feel more comfortable and confident while you're networking is to avoid situations that could cause you to feel nervous or uneasy. One situation to avoid is showing up fashionably late to a networking function, or any function for that matter. Here is the challenge: When you show up late for an event, the room is typically filled with people who arrived on time and have been chatting for some time. They have warmed up and are now networking machines. You, on the other hand, might walk into the room feeling very uncomfortable because not only are there so many unfamiliar people, but those you do know are already in deep conversation with others. Not a great situation, is it?

The best way to avoid this nerve-racking situation is to show up for any and all functions 15 minutes early. I know, I know. Only the geeky people show up early, right? Not true. I prefer to believe the adage, "the early bird gets the worm." By arriving early, you get to meet the people who put on the event before they are inundated with other guests. These are typically the movers and shakers of the organization and they are the best people to connect with, especially if you are new to the organization.

You also can start networking with a few people instead of 100. It's hard to walk into a room filled with people and move right into your networking mode. By arriving early, you can warm up slowly and so can the people you're talk-ing to. They'll appreciate that!

Last but definitely not least, you get the best choice of food and avoid the lines. Okay, this might not be the best reason, but it is important just the same. Everyone likes to eat at a networking function. Some eat because they're hungry, others because they're nervous. If you dine early, you won't have a plate in your hand when you're meeting and connecting with others. It's just one more thing you can do to get comfortable.

✔ Action Plan:

Starting _____, I will arrive at all network-ing functions at least 15 minutes early.

Leave your four-color brochures at the office.

Q. My company just spent a fortune on beautiful four-color brochures. I can't wait to attend my next function so I can put them on the literature table. Because I attend so many functions, how do I decide when to bring them?

Dave: I have never understood why people bring their best four-color glossy brochures to a networking function. Do you know why most people pick these up? Because they are filled with valuable information about your company and contain all the contact information they need to sell *you their* product or service. In other words, you have just spent $4 for someone to sell to you. Doesn't make much sense, does it?

No matter how beautiful or expensive your company brochure might be, very few people will ever buy your product or service because of it. People are not going to pick up your brochure and say, "Oh my gosh! This is the nicest brochure I have ever seen! I have to buy this product! Here's my check!" If this were the case, everyone would produce a fancy brochure, fire all their salespeople, and retire to Tahiti.

If you want to bring information to a networking function, have a professional flyer created by your local copy shop. With all of the graphic design software available today, you can create a beautiful flyer that will catch people's attention and not cost you a fortune. Print your flyer on a colorful piece of paper to draw attention to it. If someone picks it up and is interested in what you do, he will call you to get more information. Once you know if this is a qualified lead, then send your fancy-schmancy, four-color glossy brochure.

✔ **Action Plan:**

From now on I will stop throwing money away by bringing my expensive brochures to networking events.

Wear your name badge on the right.

Q. I never know what side to wear my name badge on. Any thoughts?

Dave: That's easy. Wear your name badge on the right side of your chest, a few inches below your shoulder, rather than the left as so many do. The reason is simple. When people shake your hand, their eyes instinctively follow your right arm all the way up directly to your name badge. By wearing it on the right side, it's easier for others to see, and more importantly, remember your name.

If you attend a lot of networking functions, invest in a professionally engraved name badge. People can read a custom-engraved badge much more easily and you can add a creative title such as, The Mortgage Maven, or The Event Goddess, or even The Networking Guy™.

You can purchase these badges at most copy shops, office supply stores, and mail box stores. They normally cost about eight to ten dollars and will help you stand out from the crowd.

✔ **Action Plan:**

Starting today, I will always wear my name badge on my right side. By _____, I will have a professionally engraved name badge.

Wait for the right moment to hand out your business card.

Q. One of the things I can't stand about networking is when someone walks up to me, introduces himself, and hands me a business card. I see so many people do this I'm starting to wonder if that's what I should be doing. Is this the way to start a conversation?

Dave: Sure, if you want to ruin a potential connection. In my experience, walking up to someone, introducing yourself, and handing out a business card is like saying, "Hi, my name is Dave. Here's my card. I really don't care anything about you. All I want to do is sell my product or service."

What's the first thing you think about when someone does that? I don't know about you, but my first reaction is, "Who the heck are you and what are you trying to sell me?" This is not the impression you want to make, especially with potential contacts.

Handing out a business card when you first meet someone is a crutch. It's much easier to let your business card speak for you than come out of your shell and share your name, company, and title. But, if you do the hard work, then wait for the proper time to exchange cards, the cards you receive will truly mean something.

✔ Action Plan:

Starting today, I will never start a conversation by handing someone my business card.

Understand business card etiquette.

Q. If I'm never supposed to hand out a card when I introduce myself, when is the appropriate time?

Dave: The best time to hand out your card is when people ask you for one. By waiting until people request your card, you have built up a desire in their minds. You have engaged them in such a way that they REALLY want one of your cards. Another reason it's good to wait is you save a fortune on business cards because you aren't giving them out to every Tom, Dick, and Harry that you meet.

Let me cover one more important fact about business cards. Your business card speaks for you when you aren't present. If you want your business card to shout, "Hey, make use of me!," then you'd better make sure it's professional and appropriately offered.

So, let's cover some business card etiquette. The Japanese, for instance, have strict rules for the presentation and acceptance of meishi, or a calling card—which fingers to use, how long to study it, what kind of questions to ask. Americans, on the other hand, generally treat a business card as they would a phone number written on a napkin. They shove it in their pockets or purses and forget about it.

Lewena Bayer and Karen Mallet, co-founders of In Good Company, offering private consultations, corporate training, and specialty programming, offer these basic business-card etiquette tips:

- Keep your cards clean and up-to-date. Don't hand out wrinkled, dirty, or smudged cards. If your telephone number or e-mail address has changed, get new cards. Scratched-out words give the impression of disorganization.

■ Do not offer your card unless someone asks for it, or you are engaged in a conversation about business. It is against the rules to hand out business cards as if you're dealing a game of poker. People appreciate individual attention. Hand out cards selectively instead of trying to pass out as many cards as you can.

■ When you receive a card, respond as though you have been given a gift. Pause to read and study the card, then comment on the design, or acknowledge the person's title.

■ When you receive a card during an initial meeting, keep it in front of you. If you happen to forget the person's name, you can glance at the card, making it easier to put the name with the face. If you must get rid of a business card, do so discreetly, or wait until you get home to sift through them and dispose of the ones you don't want.

Thank you Aleigh Acerni from the Charleston Regional Business Journal.

As a professional speaker, I am my product. For this reason, my card has my picture on it. Every time I give it out, I am giving away part of myself. I want to make sure the people who receive my card truly desire it, appreciate it, and are grateful for it. This might sound a bit egotistical, but if you treat your card with more respect, other people will too.

✔ Action Plan:

Starting today, I will only offer my cards to people who ask me for one.

At networking functions, talk about what you enjoy.

Q. I have a confession to make: I hate my job. Until I find another one, I'm here. My boss pushes me to attend networking functions. If I go, do I have to talk business?

Dave: The short answer is no, even though most people feel they have to talk business at a business networking function.

What do you enjoy talking about? Your job, or all of the things you like to do outside of business? Most people prefer talking about their hobbies, vacations, families, goals, dreams, and desires.

Are you unprofessional if you don't talk business at a networking function? No way! Most people are thrilled when allowed the chance to talk about things they really care about—the things they have the greatest passion for. Plus, if you can't connect your business with theirs, you'd better come up with something else to talk about very quickly, or these could be very short conversations. I have made more connections with others based on their hobbies and outside interests than I have on their jobs.

People do business with people, not companies. Think about your accountant. If she decided to work for another firm, would you just say, "It's no big deal, just assign me another accountant?" I strongly doubt it. You would follow her, because of the relationship and the connection you spent so many years developing.

If you don't like my accountant example, think about the person who cuts your hair. If your hair stylist changed salons, would you follow her? I'm sure you would. Looking at my picture, you can see that getting my hair cut isn't a big deal, since I have so little of it. Yet, when my hair stylist changed salons, I began driving more than 40 minutes each way to see her. Why? Is she is the only person who can make me look good? Nope! It's because of the relationship I have formed with her over the past 15 years.

Attending networking sessions means taking the time to learn about the person behind the business card. If all you ever talk about is business, you'll have a much harder time developing relationships with others. We aren't what we do for a living. Find out who a person really is, not just what they do, and there's a much greater likelihood that you'll create a solid connection. This is one of the most important points in my book. Please reread this last paragraph so you will *never* forget this point. You'll be glad you did!

✔ Action Plan:

Starting today, I will spend more time talking about topics that I enjoy as well as business.

Make the effort to know others, even if you don't see the connection.

Q. When I meet people at networking functions who I have nothing in common with, and will probably never do business with, is it okay to just brush them off?

Dave: In that situation, you have a choice to make. You can either blow them off and potentially miss out on some great relationships, or you can make the effort to create a connection and see what happens.

It's important to remember that every person you meet is at the head of a long line of potential relationships for you, because not only do you meet that person, you have the chance to connect with every person in his network. If you are short-sighted, you might only see the person you are talking to and miss out on the chance to connect with many more people. Plus, others might see you blowing people off and avoid approaching you for fear of getting blown off, too.

The individuals you meet are the gatekeepers to their networks. If you get past the gatekeeper, you will find more connections and more business than ever before. However, until you satisfy the gatekeeper, you won't get anywhere.

Think about your network. Would you let someone you don't know or trust have access to your friends and family? I think not. I'm a perfect example. If people don't take the time to connect with me, they are missing out on a potential relationship with any of the 2,500 people I have in my network.

Visualize the hundreds of people behind every person you meet and take the time to help the person at the head of the line.

✔**Action Plan:**

Starting today, I will remember that everyone I meet is the gatekeeper to their own extensive network of contacts.

Follow up with the people you meet.

Q. I have gone to lots of networking events, have met many people, and have collected a large stack of business cards. What do I do now?

Dave: The real success of a networking function is how well you follow up with the people you meet. You might end up with a handful of cards. A lot of these cards will be meaningless because you really don't know anything about the people who gave them to you. Focus on the cards given to you by people you learned more about than just what they do and what they would like to sell you.

Here's what I suggest: Divide your cards into two piles. In the first pile—let's call this pile A—place the cards you received without asking. In the other pile—pile B—place the cards you requested.

With pile A, since you don't really have a connection, follow up with a generic e-mail that says something like:

> Dear Jane:
>
> It was a pleasure meeting you at the Anytown Chamber function last night. I thought the program was very good and will probably attend another one in the very near future. I hope you enjoyed it too. If there is anything I can do to help you with your networking (or whatever you can help them with), please give me a call. Take care.
>
> Sincerely,
> Dave Sherman
> The Networking Guy™

To save myself from writer's (or typer's) cramp, I normally cut and paste the e-mail for each individual and send it out.

For those in pile B, send a similar e-mail, but mention any specific part of the conversation you had to spark her memory of you. You could also add some sort of action line such as, "I will call you this week to discuss_____," or, "Please call me at XXX-XXXX to chat more about _____." This e-mail should look something like this:

> Dear Jane:
>
> It was a pleasure meeting you at the Anytown Chamber function last night. I thought the program was very good and will probably attend another one in the very near future. I hope you enjoyed it too.
>
> I really enjoyed our conversation about how networking functions have changed over the years (or whatever your conversation was about). You made me think about a lot of things. I thank you for that.
>
> I'd love to get together some time for a cup of coffee. I will call you the first of next week to set up a time. If there is anything I can do to help you with your networking (or whatever you can help them with), please give me a call. I look forward to seeing you again soon. Take care.
>
> Sincerely,
> Dave Sherman
> The Networking Guy™

This e-mail didn't take very long to write, but the impact of it will help create a deeper connection with Jane, or anyone else you follow up with.

If you prefer the more traditional form of follow-up, such as note cards sent by snail mail, use the same format. However, while a mailed note card might be a bit more personal, an e-mail is faster to send and makes it much easier for the recipient to respond. Regardless, remember that deep, long-lasting connections are seldom created while you're networking. This takes place through good follow-up.

✔ **Action Plan:**

After the next event I attend I will follow up with _____ people.

Dealing With the Fear of Networking

Ask for help when attending a networking group for the first time.

Q. What about when you're new, attending for the first time? I don't know anyone and I'm not sure what to do. How do I deal with this?

Dave: When was the last time a server at a restaurant told you she was new and asked you to please bear with her? Did you immediately throw down your napkin in anger and demand to be moved to another table with a more experienced server? Of course not. You probably reassured her you would be patient and helpful while she learned the ropes.

It's the same with networking. Tell the people at the registration table you are a new attendee, or a new member to the group. This is the easiest way to start feeling more comfortable. Just walk up to the registration desk and say, "Hi, my name is Dave and this is my first time here. Is there someone I can talk to, to find out more about your group and how to possibly become a member?" I promise, someone will show up in less than 60 seconds.

A networking group succeeds by increasing its membership. It will do whatever it can to make sure you are taken care of. I have been a greeter, or what some organizations call an ambassador, at many networking functions. As a greeter, it was my job to show guests or new members how things were done and introduce them around so they didn't feel left out.

The organization's leaders will usually go out of their way to help you feel more comfortable and connected. The more comfortable you feel, the more success you will experience, and the more success you experience, the more likely you will attend more meetings and encourage your friends and associates to come. Telling people you are new also is a great icebreaker. So let them know you're new and enjoy the attention you receive.

✔ Action Plan:

Starting today and for as long as I need to, I will let people know that I am a first-timer at this network event.

Kick fear to the sidelines with a little knowledge.

Q. Where does my fear of networking in general come from, and what can I do about it?

Dave: Fear is a good news-bad news kind of thing. First, the bad news: Fear of networking is the number one reason most people don't network, so expecting to be afraid is the first step. Conquering that fear is the second.

Brian Tracy, who I have mentioned, is quite possibly one of the greatest speakers I know. He did a study on fear and learned that fear can be humankind's greatest enemy.

Look at what happened on September 11, 2001, when we lost the World Trade Center. This horrific tragedy killed thousands of people. I personally thought the equally great tragedy was the stake of fear it drove through the hearts of so many Americans. We started questioning whether the things we had done all our lives were still safe to do. I'm glad to see we have shaken off a lot of that fear, but we still have work to do.

Fear undermines self-confidence. We start to doubt our own natural abilities and question whether we can actually do what we say we can. You can't walk into a networking function, an appointment, or anywhere else for that matter, without believing in your abilities. If you don't believe in yourself, how will others believe in you?

Fear also paralyzes action. It prevents us from doing the things we need to do the most. Do you have tasks sitting on your desk right now you've wanted to accomplish, but haven't because you're afraid of the outcome? I know I do. To help overcome this habit, I have a note on my desk that says, "Do the thing you fear the most, first thing every single day."

When you ignore those things you fear, you only create stress, anxiety, loss of sleep, and much more. Consider the story about the person who used to eat a worm first thing every morning. People would look at him in disgust and ask, "Why would you do that?" He would respond, "Because it's the worst thing that could happen to me all day, and everything from that point on will be better." This is why you want to get those difficult things out of the way first.

Now the good news: According to Carl Sagan, a famous astronomer and professor at Cornell University, we are born with only two fears: the fear of falling and the fear of loud noises. All other fears are learned. If you are a parent, how many times have you said, "Don't do that. Get away from there. Be careful. Stop running with that butcher knife?" (Maybe the last one's just me.) I tell my kids the same things. We teach them to fear the things we want them to stay away from, and someone did that for you.

The good news is these learned fears can be unlearned. How? Through education. We learn that many of the things we are afraid of aren't really that scary in the first place. Fear and ignorance can be countered with knowledge and desire. The more you wish to conquer your fears, the easier it is.

Everyone is afraid of something. Everyone. No matter how self-confident, well dressed, or successful someone appears, there is fear.

Over the past few years, I have surveyed more than 5,000 workshop participants and asked them to tell me what they fear about networking? These people were CEOs, presidents, business owners, and employees. The list of fears is extensive.

Here's what I would like you to do. Read through the list and see which fears apply to you. Make check marks in this book, on a piece of paper, or just keep score on your fingers. That's one of the many reasons the big guy upstairs gave them to us.

First, let me explain the first two. The big hitter syndrome is when you are afraid the person you wish to meet is too important, popular, or famous to take the time to talk to you. For example, let's say you have a product or service that would be perfect for Bill Gates, head of Microsoft and the richest man in the world, but don't approach him at a function because you think he's a somebody and you're a nobody. That's the big hitter syndrome.

The fraud factor is when you fear you know less than the people to whom you are selling your product or service.

All of us have been rookies at one time or another. When a company hires you, you receive all of the training programs, manuals, role playing, and education you need, and then get that gentle kick in the butt to go out and produce.

Remember that first appointment? Even with all the training, it was hard to sit in front of people and persuade them to purchase a product or service from you they probably know more about than you did. That's the fraud factor.

List of Networking Fears

- The big hitter syndrome
- The fraud factor
- Fear of appearing too pushy
- Fear of talking too much
- Fear of not asking the right questions
- Fear of being judged unfairly
- Fear of not knowing what to say
- Fear of not knowing what not to say
- Fear of having nothing interesting to say
- Fear of saying something stupid
- Fear of approaching new people
- Fear of appearing too needy
- Fear of not knowing how to break the ice
- Fear of bumping into competitors
- Fear of failure

And the number one fear on the hit parade:

- Fear of rejection

How'd ya do? In all the years I've presented this list, only three people have checked them all. More importantly, less than two percent checked none of them.

What does this tell you? At least nine of every ten people suffer from some sort of fear or discomfort about networking. The average number is three to five. However, it's not the number that's important, but the fact that almost everyone else has some level of discomfort at a networking function.

This is a very powerful concept because you can now say to yourself, "I'm a little nervous, I'm a little uncomfortable, but I know that 90 percent of the people in this room are just as nervous as I am." This automatically puts you ahead. You can walk in feeling empowered and know that if you help them overcome their nervousness, they will feel more connected to you.

✔ Action Plan:

Starting with the next event I attend, I will recite the following statement before walking into any networking function:

I am feeling a bit nervous or uncomfortable right now but I'm not the only one. I know that over 90 percent of all the people here are feeling some level of discomfort, too. I will do what I can to make myself feel more comfortable and try to make others feel more comfortable as well.

Make the decision to be a fearless networker.

Q. Even though you say everyone is fearful of something when it comes to networking, I'm still a nervous wreck when I walk into a business or social function. Any specific ideas on how I can overcome this?

Dave: First, make the decision you are going to be a fearless networker. Okay, maybe not fearless, but a whole lot more comfortable than you have been. With this decision, you create the desire within yourself to be a powerful networking professional, and are now ready to conquer your fears.

Next, start talking. Start talking to everyone, everywhere! I'm talking grocery store lines, bank lines, while you're waiting to board an airplane, anywhere. It isn't difficult. Just smile and make a friendly comment. While you're at the bank, mention to the person close to you how nice or how horrible the weather is. If you're waiting to board a plane, comment on the lengthy security process you just went through. Always remember to start with a smile because a smile makes you more approachable and more friendly.

When you talk to strangers, you give them permission to talk to you. It doesn't really matter what you say. You learn to feel more comfortable talking to strangers through practice. You are helping others feel more comfortable as well.

I also suggest you start having conversations with who I like to call non-threatening individuals. These include your UPS person, your bank teller, and your next-door neighbor. I used to suggest your postal carrier, but over the past few years, some of them have become a bit more threatening. Still, most postal carriers are kind, peaceful people.

These people have no impact on the success or failure of your life, and are therefore easy to practice with. One of my favorites is talking to people in the elevator. I have had some of my nicest chats inside that little eight foot square.

Elevators are very stressful. Everyone is trapped in a very small space they can't leave until the doors open. Most people welcome the chance to lessen the stress by talking. When I start talking, the first thing they do is smile because they're so thrilled someone has spoken and released some of the pressure. Once they're smiling, they'll talk about almost anything. Here are some phrases you might use to initiate a conversation:

- How is your day going?

- Are you glad it's Friday? (Make sure it is really Friday before you use this line. It freaks people out if you use that line on Tuesday.)

- Why do people always look at the floor or stare at the numbers when riding in an elevator?

What you say isn't the issue. Saying something is all it takes to reduce the stress in an elevator and have a nice chat too.

One warning: Please don't attempt this until you start to feel totally comfortable talking to people everywhere. One wrong statement to a stranger in an elevator and you could be scarred for life! Well, maybe not for life, but you will start to question whether talking to anyone is a good idea. Take it from The Networking Guy™: If you practice this skill, you will become a very powerful networker.

✔ **Action Plan:**

I will initiate conversations with _____ people today.

Be prepared with effective opening lines.

Q. I appreciate the tips on how to speak to just about anyone, but how do I start the conversation?

Dave: Being prepared with a few opening lines will help you overcome this discomfort, which, by the way, is probably the number one thing that causes nervousness, angst, butterflies, *shpilkes* (Yiddish for nervous), or whatever else you call it. Don't feel bad. It's not easy for veteran networkers either, including me.

Sometimes, after you introduce yourself and say what you do and listen to what the other person does, the conversation stalls. This is where the discomfort begins. This also is the perfect time to use one of those great opening lines. What! You don't have any? Here are four of the world's greatest icebreakers. Okay, they might not be the world's greatest, but they always work like a charm:

- "What do you like to do when you're not working?" This simple question is the best way to create conversation. You give people permission to start talking about non-business topics, and for this, they will be grateful. Listen closely to the answer, because the first thing they mention is usually where their greatest passion lies, whether it's golf, travel, or family. Whatever it is, it's the thing they love talking about most. These conversations create the best connections. The more you learn about their hobbies, families, and dreams, the greater the likelihood for a deep connection.

■ "How did you get into your current business?" People love sharing the details of how they started their own business, or how they were selected for their current position. However, just know that once people get started, it's tough to get them to stop.

■ "Hi, I'm Dave, and I have never been to this function before. Have you?" Honesty like this always works and can produce great results. People who have attended that specific event before will more than likely go out of their way to make sure you are comfortable and enjoying yourself. On the other hand, if they're new, you can support each other in learning about the group. No one likes to be alone at a new event. The sooner you start initiating conversations, the sooner you'll start connecting and feel more comfortable and confident.

■ "Have you ever been to (this venue) before?" Opening lines like this address your shared reality. What is shared reality? The space you are sharing, the paintings on the walls, the view from the window, or the food at the buffet. Other opening lines include, "Did you try the Swedish meatballs?," or "What a beautiful view from here." Always check out the space so you can be prepared with a great shared-reality comment.

There are dozens of things you can say to initiate conversation. Read the newspaper or watch the news before you attend an event and you will always be able to create conversation with just about anyone.

✔Action Plan:

I will use one of the above mentioned ice breakers to start a conversation with someone I don't know by _____.

Make connections face-to-face.

Q. I have made some very good friends through e-mail. Since I tend to be shy, is it possible to create a powerful network through e-mail?

Dave: I don't believe so. To make a real connection with someone, it's important you meet face-to-face. If your only connection is through e-mail, you might not get the best or most honest impression. Once you have met and started to create a solid connection, you can use e-mail to build the relationship.

While it might seem your e-mail network is there for you, when you're really in a bind, you need people you can call on at a moment's notice. E-mail is a wonderful method of communication, but it will never replace the connections you make with people face to face.

✔ Action Plan:

Starting today, I will build my connections with others by meeting them face to face.

Get a networking buddy and do P.R. for each other at events.

Q. I am a very timid person and networking doesn't come easy for me. A friend of mine is always dragging me to networking events and we normally end up talking to each other the whole evening. I would like to meet a few people. Any thoughts on how my friend and I can connect with others?

Dave: Patricia Fripp is one of the greatest speakers I have ever heard. She's a ball of fire who speaks with such energy and passion that, after hearing her, you feel like you can take on the world. She wrote an article addressing your question. Here's an excerpt:

Travel With Your Own P.R. Agent Technique

Here's what you can do. Enlist a co-sales professional, friend, or fellow speaker to form a duo. My networking buddy in San Francisco is Susan RoAne. When we arrive at an event, we alternately separate and come together. I'll walk up to Susan as she is talking to someone, and she'll say, "Larry, let me introduce you to Patricia Fripp. Patricia is truly one of the greatest speakers in the country." And, I will turn around and say, "Larry, I bet Susan is too modest to tell you she's the best-selling author of three books."

When you do this, just as RoAne and I do, you're saying great things about each other that you'd love your prospects to know, but modesty prevents you from telling them.

Suppose Natalie and Fred are secret partners. As Fred walks up, Natalie says to the person she's been talking to, "Jack, I'd like you to meet Fred. Fred has taught me nearly everything I know about sales and our product line. There has never been a sales contest in our company he hasn't won." Then, Fred can say, "Well, Natalie's being very generous. It's true; I've been with our company for 16 years. But, Natalie's been here for only six months, and she's brought in more new business than any other person in the 53-year history of our firm, so she knows a couple of things too. I tell you, you couldn't do better than work with someone as enthusiastic as Natalie."

Patricia and her friend work together to look great to others. To learn more about Patricia, you can reach her at 1-800-634-3035. Her Web site is www.fripp.com and her e-mail address is Pfripp@fripp.com

---

✔ **Action Plan:**

By _____ I will find a networking buddy.

What Do I Say and How Do I Say It?

31 Keep your introduction to ten seconds.

Q. I've heard I need to keep my introduction to ten seconds, but I never understood why. What's the rush?

Dave: Three reasons:

- Most people are very impatient. If you don't believe me, think about the last time you or someone you know waited impatiently for the timer on the microwave oven to ring. We cook food three-to-five times faster than ever before, and it's still not fast enough. We used to go to the library to do research. Now, we get on the Internet in the comfort of our own homes and complain when it takes 41 seconds to download a 126-page book. If you can't tell what you do quickly, people will stop listening to you!

- Most people easily lose interest. Need an example? I have more than 300 TV channels at home—38 movie channels, 11 sports channels, and more news channels than I could ever watch. Why do I need that many channels? Because, if one channel doesn't grab my interest in 6.3 seconds, I can flip to another. I have more than 100 channels on my car radio for the same reason. I would need to drive from Phoenix to Los Angeles to hear one song on each station. If you don't get to your point quickly, people will stop listening to you!

- People are very busy. We are working more hours and schlepping our kids around more than ever before. Did you know that 70 percent of Americans have a second job or a business on the side? With obligations like these, if you don't cut to the chase, people will stop listening to you!

Your introduction must grab attention quickly to be effective. Once you craft a good ten-second introduction, you will start to hear the three most beautiful words you can hear: Tell me more!

✔ Action Plan:

By _____, I will create a better way to introduce myself to people and hold their attention.

Give people a reason to listen to your introduction.

Q. I firmly believe you only get one chance to make a great first impression. When I meet people and introduce myself, is it important to tell them my name, my title, and the company I work for?

Dave: I hate to be the one to break this to you, but no one really cares who you are, what you do, or where you work! I don't mean to be harsh or disrespectful. What I want you to understand is that until you give people a reason to listen to you, they won't!

Why aren't the above three pieces of information enough? Let's start with your name. I'm sure you have a great name you are very proud of. It might have a long history, or even come from the old country. However, if a name was so important, why do most people forget it within 15 seconds of being introduced? Because they have no reason to remember it. You haven't shown how you can make an impact on their lives.

Now, let's bash your title a bit. Take a minute, stop reading, and recite your job title out loud. What do you think? Do you like it? Most people don't, even those who give it to themselves. Does it say anything about what you really do? That's doubtful. Is your title skills-based or ego-based? Most titles are ego-based—more a designation than a real title. I know a gentleman who works for himself and has no employees. His title is president and CEO. This is the ultimate ego trip. Most titles are meaningless because they are assigned to the position, not the person. However, the position isn't out there making connections. You are!

To hammer this point home, I invite you to join me in the Anti-Title Oath. Please raise your right hand and read the following out loud:

> I, (state your name), solemnly swear I will never, I mean NEVER, recite my title when someone asks me what I do for a living, until the end of time, or the Cubbies win the World Series.

Now that I've insulted your name and title, I'll take aim at your company. Unless you work for a very large company everyone on earth has heard of, no one cares. Please don't take offense. I'm only sharing the facts. Why don't they care? They have no reason to be impressed.

Do you know what WIIFM stands for? It means What's In It For Me? Until you answer this question, 99.9 percent of the people in this world will not care who you are, what your title is, or who you work for.

Instead, learn to deliver a killer ten-second introduction. Here are a few tips:

- The next time you're asked what you do, take about a half-second to hear the question as, "What do you do that will directly benefit me or make my life easier?" People want to know what they are going to get from working with you. When you cut to the chase and let them know, they will listen to you.

- When asked what you do, limit your answer to one thing. You might have many products and services, but if, like many rookie networkers, you try to tell people everything you do in ten seconds, you'll just confuse them. While you think it sounds impressive, they can't remember any of it.

To select that one thing, think of the three most popular products or services your company offers and pick the one that has the widest appeal to your current audience. If you present that one product or service in the right way, you will engage listeners and they will want to know more.

■ Talk about the benefits. When asked about their business, 99 out of 100 people will recite all the features they offer. The fact is, no one cares about the features. People care about how these features will benefit them.

Do you know the difference between a feature and a benefit? According to *Merriam Webster's Dictionary*, a feature is a prominent part, a characteristic, or a special attraction of something or someone. A benefit is an act of kindness or something that promotes well-being. Which of these would be more important to you? Features are what your company provides and benefits are what your customers receive.

I used to sell advertising for a weekly newspaper in Phoenix. The company taught me to focus on features and benefits. Once I learned more about people, I now only focus on benefits, benefits, benefits.

Here are a few examples:

✔ "Our company can help you save time and money." Great for a consultant and almost anyone selling a service.

✔ "We help take the worry out of doing your taxes." Great for an accountant or CPA.

✔ "I can show you how to buy the home of your dreams." Great for a realtor or lender.

✔ "I can show you how to network with more comfort and more success." This line can only be used by the one and only Networking Guy!

The next time someone asks you what you do, focus on the benefit you can bring and you will be amazed at how many more people will respond.

■ Once you know the benefits, determine how those benefits affect your listener emotionally.

Think about the way people buy things. Do they purchase products and services based purely on intellect? No way! If that were true, no one ever would have bought the Pet Rock, Pokemon cards, the GMC Pacer, or thousands of other products. People buy with their hearts. Those who can pull the heart strings will always succeed. For example:

✔ "I help protect your most valuable assets—your family." Perfect for a security company or alarm company.

✔ "I can help you look as young as you feel." Perfect for beauty product sales.

✔ "I show people how to out drive all their golf buddies." Perfect for a club manufacturer or golf pro.

When you focus on the core reason for buying—emotions—your clients will respond to you more quickly.

■ Keep your answer to the question "What do you do?" as simple as possible. If people don't understand, they not only can't help you, you've made them feel less intelligent. This is not how great connections are made. They will never stop the conversation and say, "Wait, wait! I didn't understand that last part. Could you please explain it to me?" They will nod up and down, pretend to care, and get out of the conversation as quickly as possible.

The simpler the message, the easier it is to create deep connections because others will know exactly how to help you.

✔**Action Plan:**

I will create a killer ten-second introduction by

_____.

Follow three steps to a great 30-second commercial.

Q. *A friend of mine took me to a chamber of commerce breakfast event. Not only did I have to be there at 6:30 a.m., I had to stand up and give a 30-second commercial in front of the entire group. I have no idea what I said, but I know I didn't like it. Is there a method to developing a great 30-second commercial?*

Dave: Yes. It is very easy to create a great 30-second commercial, or elevator speech, if you know the steps.

Most people ramble when they present a 30-second commercial. It would be better if they didn't do a commercial at all. Rambling makes you look unprofessional, and no one wants that. For a powerful 30-second commercial, follow these three steps:

- Step 1. Grab your listener's attention as quickly as possible. The audience might have already heard 30 to 40 commercials before you deliver yours. If you don't snap them back to attention, they'll never hear you. Here are a few examples:

    ✔ Company A sells custom embroidered shirts: "When you walked into your office today, how was your staff dressed? Did they look as professional as you would like them to look?"

    ✔ Company B sells services to home-based businesses: "How many of you own home-based businesses? Have you found that companies that offer the business services you need are so busy chasing the big fish that they never pay any attention to your needs?"

✔ Company C sells insurance: "What would happen if a drunk driver ran a red light and slammed into your car, seriously injuring you? How would your family get by during your long recovery period?"

■ Step 2. Once you have their attention, offer an agreement statement. An agreement statement starts people thinking they need your product or service long before you ever try to sell it to them. This is a statement that will get their heads nodding up and down, while they're saying to themselves, "Yeah, I do need that." Consider these:

✔ "Wouldn't it be nice if everyday you saw your staff, you said to yourself, man, they look good today?"

✔ "Wouldn't it be great if you found a company that specializes in business services designed for home-based businesses?"

✔ "Wouldn't you like to know that your family will be well taken care, even when you can't do it yourself?"

■ Step 3. This is the best part. After you have their attention and they're nodding up and down, you get to be the hero of your own commercial. Ta da ta da!

Start your closing line with the following, "Well, my name is (your name) with (whatever the name of your company is), and..." add your killer ten-second introduction. This is your tag line. The catchier the tag line, the more people will remember you. For example:

✔ "My name is John Smith with XYZ Corp and I can help make your staff look that great every single day. Please come see me for more information. Thank you."

✔ "My name is Sally with ABC Corp. and I am the home-based business owner's very best friend. Come find out how I can help you. Thank you."

✔ "My name is Sam with LMNOP Insurance and it's my job to help take care of your family when you can't. Come see me afterwards to see how I can help you too. Thank you."

If you follow these three simple steps, you can develop a 30-second commercial that will get results. It takes time to perfect this process, but you'll notice instant results the first time you use it.

✔ Action Plan:

I will create a terrific 30-second commercial by

_____.

34

Avoid the elevator speech don'ts.

Q. I am working on my elevator speech. I think it's coming along great but are there things I should avoid saying to make sure it really rocks?

Dave: Yes, there are certain things you want to avoid in your commercial. Here are a few of them:

- Avoid starting your commercial by saying "Hi, my name is (your name) and I work for (your company)." Every time I hear that, I want to stand up and scream, "Who cares?!" Until you have grabbed their attention, most people don't really care who you are, or who you work for... yet! Save that for the end, when people will want to know.

- Avoid giving your phone number, address, or your e-mail address. If you had gone to as many networking functions as I have, you would notice that 99 percent of the people don't take notes. If people don't remember names, they won't remember addresses.

- Never wing it. If there is only one tip you embrace, please let it be this one. Always know what you are going to say before you say it. One of the best ways to overcome nervousness is to practice, practice, practice. If you know what you're going to say, you'll sound more convincing and be much more effective.

- Don't lose track of time. A 30-second elevator speech is supposed to be 30 seconds. It never looks good when you have to stop mid-sentence because you've gone over your time limit. If you prepare properly, you can deliver an effective and powerful message in 30 seconds or less.

■ If you are especially uncomfortable speaking in public, don't do another 30-second commercial until you find a local Toastmasters chapter. You need to address this fear-of-public-speaking issue as soon as possible. If you really want to get good at delivering a powerful 30-second elevator speech, Toastmasters is the best place to learn. Even if you have no intention of becoming a public speaker, Toastmasters will help you feel more confident when networking, more effective when speaking, and more successful in whatever business you're in. Visit www.toastmasters.org for more information.

✔ Action Plan:

By _____, I will find a Toastmasters chapter and attend at least one meeting.

Specific Networking Techniques

35

To find a new job, focus on the benefits you bring.

Q. I was just notified that I am being laid off at the end of the month. I've heard most of the good jobs are never listed in the paper. How do I network my way to a great job?

Dave: A very good friend of mine was laid off during a bad economy from a job she had held for eight years. Here's how I helped her. I sent an e-mail to my network of about 2,500 people, and within 24 hours had received more than 200 e-mails and 25 phone calls from people looking to help my friend. From those responses emerged 80 job openings, many from well-known companies. She ultimately decided to take a great position with a local company that provided her with even better pay and benefits than her previous employer.

More than 70 percent of all jobs in this country are found through networking. Here are three ways to make your networking more effective, more productive, and more successful—and be back to work soon.

- Always use the KISS method: Keep It Short and Simple. So often I hear information that is so complicated or full of industry jargon, I don't have a clue what they need, especially with high-tech positions. What might seem elementary to you could go right over the heads of most listeners, many of whom may have valuable resources available to you. To make matters worse, very few people will ever ask you to explain yourself. They don't like to admit they don't understand. It makes them feel less intelligent.

- In the movie, *Philadelphia*, Denzel Washington's character always asked the opposing attorneys to explain it to him like he was a five-year-old. The point is, if a five-year-old can understand your explanation, everyone else can too.

- When potential employers ask you to tell them about yourself, spend your time focusing on why they should hire you instead of your educational background, employment history, or all of the other things that are important to you. While that might seem to be the best response to "Tell me about yourself," it's the last thing you want to say.

- Let me break something to you: No matter how impressive your background is, nobody cares... yet. A potential employer wants to know what benefit you can bring to the organization. In other words, the WIIFM response "What's in it for me?" Grab the most attention by talking about what's in it for other people. When you address how you can fulfill their needs, they will pay more attention to your needs.

- Focus on one specific area, position, or industry when sharing what you're looking for.

Most people believe the more information they provide, the easier it will be for others to help. Unfortunately, the opposite is usually true. People can only process so much information at one time. If you bombard them, they'll get confused and won't be able to help you.

Provide examples of companies you're interested in, such as American Express, Dial Corp., Microsoft, or one of my favorites, Krispy Kreme. Identify a couple of specific jobs you would like, such as sales manager, account executive, customer service representative, or again, one of my favorites, official doughnut taster. With a clear picture of the job you really want, they will have a much stronger desire to help you.

Finding a good job isn't easy. By following these simple steps, you should be able to find that next great job with less effort, less stress, and more success.

✔ **Action Plan:**

I am looking for a job, so starting today, I will let people know what I can do for them instead of focusing on all the things I need or want in a job.

✔ **Action Plan:**

I am not currently looking for a job, but I will call or e-mail people I know who are and pass along this tip.

36

Be sensitive and respectful of others when chatting on airplanes.

Q. I travel a lot for my business. I have many opportunities to talk to the person I'm sitting next to, but I never know what to say or do? What is the best way to network across the friendly skies?

Dave: Picture this: you are sitting peacefully waiting for your plane to take off. The seat next to you is empty and you're hoping it stays that way. Just as the flight attendants are about to close the door, one more passenger rushes in and sits down right next to you.

Once settled, he turns to you and says, "Boy, this plane sure is jammed," or "I thought that security line would never end," or, one of my favorites, "Are you traveling for business or pleasure?" Even though you try to end the conversation, your talkative neighbor keeps rambling. You are either forced to carry on a conversation with a total stranger who can't take a hint, or remove yourself from the situation. This is one of your worst nightmares.

As a professional speaker who travels often, I have run into this many times. You might think as The Networking Guy™ I would be one of those chatty passengers. I promise you, I am not. I do, however, believe you can network on an airplane without forcing the other passengers to leap out of the plane to escape you. Here are a few ways to connect with fellow passengers without torturing them:

- ■ Test the water before you dive in. Start a casual conversation with a simple comment like, "Boy, they don't leave you much room for your knees these days," and see what happens. If you get a friendly comment, or any comment that continues the conversation, the individual wants to continue chatting. If, instead, you get a look that says he thinks you're some sort of alien from another planet, that's a good signal to pull out your book or laptop and entertain yourself.

- Keep the other passenger happy by asking lots of questions. The more the other person talks, the better conversationalist she will think you are. Ask her where she lives, whether she is traveling for business or pleasure, or what her favorite hobby is. By connecting through non-business topics, it becomes much easier to start a business conversation. You are no longer just a person with a business card, but someone with whom your seat mate might have something in common.

- Watch for warning signs. Keep your eyes and ears open for signals the other passenger wants to end your fascinating chat. If he starts looking at his book or magazine, this might be his way of saying, "I've talked enough and I'd like to read now." Don't take this as an insult. While I'm sure you are a fabulous conversationalist, people like to read, sleep, work, or stare into space when they are on airplanes. Perhaps you'd like to end the conversation. That's okay. Many times, I have said, "It's been nice talking to you, but I need to get some work done." It works every time, and I have never upset anyone.

- If you do find yourself in a lengthy conversation, make sure you turn your entire body toward the person to whom you are speaking. Not only does this show your interest, it prevents that uncomfortable "crick" you get when you keep your head turned to one side for too long.

I have met some fascinating people on airplanes, and had some great conversations. I also have had my share of horrible ones. A good conversation can make an eight-hour flight seem like two. A bad one can make two hours feel like a lifetime. Chatting with you will be enjoyable if you follow a few simple ground rules to make the conversation as pleasant for the other person as possible.

✔ Action Plan:

The next time I travel, I will start a conversation with someone sitting next to me on a plane and remember to use these ideas.

Check out the situation before joining an existing group's conversation.

Q. When I walk into a networking function, everyone seems to be chatting away in small groups of four to six people. Sometimes I'm interested in a group's conversation and would like join it. How do I join a small group of people who are chatting casually?

Dave: The best way to join a group is to slowly approach and listen for the topic. If it interests you, walk right up and ask if you can join in. They will almost always say yes. Introduce yourself, but don't, under any circumstances, attempt to take over the conversation. You are like a guest who needs to spend some time listening before you can contribute to the conversation.

There are some groups you should avoid. If a group of two or three is talking quietly and really paying attention to each other, leaning in toward each other while talking, or their faces are less than three feet away, this group does not want to be disturbed.

On the other hand, if you are having a casual conversation and notice others standing just outside your group listening but not approaching, take a step back and invite them to join you. Many people are too timid to approach a group of relative strangers and ask to join in. It is then your job to reach out to them. They will feel more welcome and comfortable and you might just start a new connection.

✔**Action Plan:**

At the next event I attend, I will approach a group of people and use these tips to join their conversation. When I am involved in a conversation, I will invite a person to come over and chat with us.

38

Memorize some key phrases to keep conversations flowing smoothly.

Q. I often meet people when I'm networking who don't say much. It's hard enough starting a conversation with a complete stranger, but it's even harder when I have to carry most of the conversation. Any suggestions?

Dave: This is one of the biggest challenges in business today. While initiating conversations with people you don't know is difficult, trying to continue the conversation with someone who doesn't say much is agony! To encourage others to participate, ask open-ended questions. These questions inspire long answers. Here are three methods of asking open-ended questions:

- Start questions with words like "what," "where," or "how." Examples include:

  ✔ How did you get into your current line of work?

  ✔ What's the best piece of advice you can offer from your industry?

  ✔ Where have you been networking lately that has provided you with the best results?

- Ask questions that naturally lead to further responses. With certain phrases, you can easily keep people talking for as long as you wish. Some examples are:

  ✔ Is what you're saying...
  ✔ You seem to be saying...
  ✔ What I hear you saying...

✔ Let me see if I understand correctly.

The above statements indicate you're interested and prepared to listen to everything they want to say. They will feel important knowing you are focusing all of your attention on them.

■ Use a response that encourages more details. The more details individuals share with you, the better you'll understand them. Some of these responses are:

✔ I see...And...So...
✔ Oh...Go on...Yes...
✔ And then...Indeed...Really...
✔ That's interesting...

These words indicate you are listening and encourage your partner to please continue.

With a little practice and preparation, you will never have to carry another conversation by yourself.

✔Action Plan:

Starting today, I will make sure to ask more open-ended questions so I can learn more about others and make them feel comfortable with the conversation.

Use memory techniques to remember names.

Q. I'm having a big problem. I always have a hard time remembering a person's name, even if I know him. Any suggestions on how I can better remember names?

Dave: While I might be The Networking Guy™, one of my greatest faults is that I'm terrible when it comes to remembering names. I never forget a face, but I have a major problem attaching the proper name to the face. Here's what often happens: When I'm busy racking my brain to come up with the person's name, I don't hear a word he's saying. This causes serious problems. If you don't listen, how can you help, or properly respond? You can't!

The reason names are so hard to remember is that they have no connection with the individuals. A hundred years ago, if you were the baker in town, you were known as John the Baker. Today, no one would know who John the Accountant is just by looking at him. However, when you approach this problem with a positive frame of mind, remembering names can be relatively simple. Try these techniques:

- Face association. Discreetly examine a person's face when you are introduced. Try to find an unusual feature. Create an association in your mind between that characteristic, the face, and the name. You might associate the person with someone you know who has the same name, or with a rhyme or image from the person's face or defining feature.

■ Repetition. When you are introduced, ask for the name to be repeated. Use the name yourself as often as possible (without overdoing it). If it's unusual, ask how it is spelled, or where it comes from, and if appropriate, exchange cards. The more often you hear and see the name, the more likely it will eventually sink in. After you have parted company, repeat the name in your mind several times. If you are particularly interested in this person, you might make a few notes.

While fairly simple, these methods are quite powerful. Creating associations with images, or other people, can substantially help name recall. It sinks in with repetition and review. The emphasis is on practice, patience, and progressive improvement.

Thank you Mind Tools, Inc.

If you happen to be one of the lucky people who remembers names, it's your obligation to make sure other people don't suffer when they forget yours. When you see someone you know who is struggling to remember your name, start the conversation like this: "Hi Mary, Dave Sherman," and reach out to shake her hand. Most likely, she will say she remembered your name, but she will be eternally grateful to you if she didn't. By making sure people know your name at the beginning of a conversation, they are more likely to listen closely to you, giving you a much better chance of creating that deeper connection.

✔ Action Plan:

Starting today, I will use these techniques to remember people's names. I will also reintroduce myself to people so I am sure they will remember my name.

Use tact and grace to disengage from long-winded conversations.

Q. I don't know what it is about me but I often find myself stuck in dull and pointless conversations. How do I break out of these uncomfortable situations without being rude or hurting someone's feelings?

Dave: You have two choices if you find yourself stuck in a long-winded conversation—the little-white-lie route or the truthful route. Both work very well. You'll need to decide which one works best for you.

- Truthful route: "Well, it's been great chatting with you. If it's okay with you, I'm going to mingle and meet some more people, plus, I don't want to take up anymore of your time. Thanks again for talking."

  This line is perfect. It's truthful, allows the other person to feel she is in control (which everyone loves to feel), and shows respect for her time. Whenever I've used this line, no one has ever said, "No, you can't go mingle." Other people feel good, and you can now enjoy your new-found freedom.

- Little-white-lie route: "Well, it's been nice talking to you, but I need to head to the restroom. Do you happen to know where it is?" After he tells you, walk away and head toward the bathroom. Even if you don't have to go, play out the situation in case he's watching you.

"Well, it's been a pleasure chatting with you, but I need to get something to drink." Head over to the refreshment area and get something to drink, or at least look like you're getting something to drink. If, by some chance, the person you are trying to break away from follows you, you'll need to try another line.

"Would you mind excusing me? I just saw someone I've been trying to talk to for a very long time. It's been a pleasure talking to you. Thanks." Then head over to someone you know in the room and start talking to that person. This is probably the best way to exit a conversation, because you are at a networking function and you want to network and connect with as many people as you can.

These techniques will help you end a conversation. Just make sure you end the conversation on a good note. You never know when the conversation might lead to a huge piece of business. Just because someone is long-winded doesn't mean he doesn't have something to say.

✔ Action Plan:

Starting at the next event I attend, I will use one of these techniques to escape from potentially endless babbling.

Stay focused to be a good listener.

Q. I know that listening is one of, if not the, most important skills in networking. While I consider myself a good listener, what can I do to improve?

Dave: Listening is an art, a skill, and a discipline, and like any other acquired ability, it is learned. You need to understand what is involved and develop the necessary techniques. To be a good listener, you learn to ignore your own needs and concentrate on the person speaking. Here are five tips to help you become a great listener:

- Maintain eye contact. Good eye contact says, "You are important to me and I want to hear what you have to say." We all know what it feels like when someone isn't paying attention. He might be looking over your shoulder, or checking out the buffet table. You might want to reach out, grab him by the clothing, and say, "Hey, I'm talking here!" To avoid being grabbed yourself, let the individual know how important he is to you by staying focused.

- Focus on the content, not the delivery. Some people are great communicators. They always seem comfortable, enunciate every word perfectly, and sound as if they know what they're talking about. Others aren't great communicators, but just because they don't speak with real authority doesn't mean they don't have valuable information to share.

  You'll never be able to tell how good a communicator someone is before you start talking to him or her. You can tell you aren't focusing on the content if you are counting the number of times a person says "um" in 15 minutes. You will be surprised at the amount of great information you can receive if you stop judging the delivery and listen to the content.

- Stay focused on the person you're talking to. This is a supreme challenge in a networking environment. It's easy to let your mind wander, or become distracted by other people in the room. If you do get distracted, immediately refocus your attention on the person you're talking to. This isn't always easy, but no one ever said listening was easy. If it were, everyone would be great at it.

- Consider each conversation a potential treasure hunt. You have no idea what could come from any conversation. It might be mindless babble, or contain a solution to a current business challenge. You'll be more engaged when you realize every conversation could provide your next great idea or solution.

- Turn off the voice in your head. Most people speak at a rate of 150 words per minute (up to 200 words a minute east of the Mississippi), and think at 700 words a minute, leaving a gap for the mind to wander. It's very difficult to stay focused, but if you do, you will hear more of what's being said.

Your mind has the capacity to listen, think, write, and ponder, all at the same time, but it does take practice. These suggestions will help you stay focused on the person's words. Listening well is not easy, but if you practice, you will connect to people more quickly.

✔ **Action Plan:**

Starting today, I will follow these tips to become a better listener.

---

42 Develop a proper handshake to make a good impression.

Q. I've heard a good handshake is one of the most impor-
tant ways to make a good first impression. Is there a
right way and a wrong way to shake hands?

Dave: A handshake is normally the first physical contact between two people. It can help create a connection or it can drive people away.

In January 1973, one month before my Bar Mitzvah (a ceremony that marks a Jewish boy's entry to adulthood within the Jewish community), my father sat me down and formally explained the proper way to shake hands. I still remember that precious moment with my dad like it was yesterday. Unfortunately, my father passed away five short years later, but this handshaking lesson lives on in me. My handshake has become one of the most recognizable aspects of my personality, so much so, it thoroughly impressed my future father-in law when I first met him.

Most people underestimate the impact of a handshake. Here are ten tips for a powerful, confident handshake:

- Always stand when you meet someone, whether you are a man or a woman.

- Face the person squarely, not at an angle.

- Make contact between your thumb and index finger, or web to web, avoiding the dead fish or finger-tip-only handshake.

- Keep thumbs straight up. Avoid rolling one hand over or under, as this can denote a power struggle.

- Make eye contact and hold the gaze throughout the introduction.

- Give a pleasant, approachable smile, not an overly big grin.

- Carry papers, briefcase, or drinks in the left hand, leaving the right hand free to shake hands.

- Do not squeeze someone's hand too hard (bone crushing), or too soft (dead fish). These are both signs of insecurity.

- Avoid pumping the hand up and down excessively.

- Whoever is being introduced extends his hand first.

(Thank you Cynthia Grosso, Charleston School of Protocol and Etiquette, Inc.)

I learn a lot about people by the way they shake hands. To make a good impression, practice that handshake and no one will ever forget you.

✔ Action Plan:

By _____, I will ask someone who knows me well for his or her honest opinion about my handshake. If it doesn't communicate the impression I want, I will improve my handshake by _____.

Write thank-you notes with the other person in mind.

Q. Can you please settle an argument I have been having with my business partner? Is it best to thank someone by e-mail, or with a hand-written note?

Dave: The choice is yours, because how you send the thank-you note is not as important as what you say in the note, and how it makes the other person feel. Let's look at the pros and cons of each.

E-mails are easier and faster to send. You just sit down and type, press the "send" key, and they arrive at their destinations in seconds while the memories of the meetings are still fresh. They're easier to save as part of your in-box, or other file, and much simpler to respond to.

While e-mail has its advantages, its biggest disadvantage is its lack of personality and warmth. Unless you use a fancy-schmancy font style, your e-mail looks like every other email. Nothing really makes your e-mail thank-you note stand out.

A written note, on the other hand, shows you really appreciated the meeting because you took the time to write the note, address the envelope, stamp it, and mail it. You can use any style of stationery and your own handwriting always looks nicer, unless you have chicken-scratch penmanship like me. The only downside to a hand-written thank-you note is how much time it takes. If you send lots of thank-you notes, you'd need hours to write them. Your assistant could write the notes, but that would defeat the purpose.

So, which is the better method? I'd say the hand-written note. It shows more thought, effort, and appreciation.

Which do I send? E-mail is the only way for me. I send at least 10 to15 thank-you e-mails a day. After a trade show or conference, I might send out 50 to 100. E-mail works because I can respond more quickly and continue to develop the connection by asking more questions, learning more about my contact, and sharing information about myself.

When I was a kid, I hated writing thank-you notes, especially if it was for a gift I'd already broken. As I grew older, I learned to understand the value of a well-written note.

✔ Action Plan:

Starting after my next event, I will send thank-you notes, whether by e-mail or snail mail, within 24 to 48 hours of the meeting.

Convince yourself you can network, and you can.

Q. There are times I need a little extra umpff to go to a networking event. Any thoughts on how I can get my butt moving?

Dave: As an avid golfer, I often need to convince myself I can hit a specific shot even when I'm not sure. Whether it's a long shot over water, or a short chip shot to a small green, I have to say to myself, "Come on Dave, you can do this! You can hit this shot! You can do it!" I usually feel so empowered after this, most of the time the ball goes exactly where it's supposed to. Am I so great I can hit any shot I want? Yeah right! I convince myself I can do it, even though I'm not sure. This is how you psyche yourself up for networking. You motivate yourself into being a great networker.

Before you leave your car to walk into a networking function, look in the rear-view mirror and repeat:

> I am a great networker. I am a fearless networker. I will do everything I can to help others and expect nothing in return. I might be nervous, but I know everyone else is too. I will go inside, meet people, and make great connections. I am a great networker. I am a fearless networker. I am a great networker!

Repeat these words once or twice before you go inside. You'll feel so empowered you won't help but succeed.

Brian Tracy once said, "Fake it until you make it." He believes if you convince yourself you're a great networker, you will be a better networker. Just keep saying to yourself, "I'm a fearless networker. I'm a fearless networker." Pump yourself up and see just how fearless you can really be.

✔ **Action Plan:**

By _____, I will write a motivational message that I will recite to myself before I walk into any networking function.

Stay in touch with your network on a regular basis with valuable information.

Q. I've probably met a thousand people over the last couple of years. I've organized all their names and contact information neatly in my computer. My question is, what the heck am I supposed to do with them? How important is it to stay in touch?

Dave: A sound network is based on long-term relationships. You need to develop a follow-up strategy to communicate with your contacts on a regular basis and keep them informed.

I frequently hear, "I know I need to stay in touch, but how do I do that without becoming a pest?" Consider these ideas and think about what you could do to keep in touch with your contacts:

- Drop a congratulatory note to someone whose name you hear or read in the media. We all like to be recognized.

- Invite your network to attend a trade show or other event you are involved in. Attendance is not the crucial issue. Your invitation demonstrates your keen desire to keep them informed.

- Send a copy of an article, or information on a pertinent Web site, if you think it might be of interest.

- Share information with your network on conferences or conventions you learn about.

- Invite your network to attend an event sponsored by your company or organization.

- Above all, be alert to opportunities that might benefit your network and recommend them to others for consideration.

Stay in touch by supplying useful information when you can. Admittedly, this requires a little imagination, time, and effort, but these steps help establish and maintain a level of trust. Consistently share valuable or useful information with your contacts and they will not only seek you out for assistance, but be receptive if you call them for help.

Thank you Reg Perie from CanadaOne Magazine.

✔ **Action Plan:**

I will stay in contact with _____ people in my networking group in the next week.

Know the networking don'ts to prevent problems.

Q. People I meet tell me all about things to do while I'm networking. Unfortunately, very few people tell me what not to do. What are your thoughts on what not to do while networking?

Dave: The list of networking faux pas is quite long, but you'll never know the reasons why unless they are explained. Here is my list of networking don'ts and why:

- Don't be a know-it-all. I have met many people who seem to have an answer for everything. No matter the topic, they always know the right way to do things. No one likes talking to people who think they know everything about everything. If you do know everything about a certain topic, feel free to share your knowledge, but let other people share their thoughts too, without you having to have the last word.

- Don't spend too much time networking with really important people, such as company CEOs, presidents, owners or even celebrities. I'm not saying you shouldn't attempt to make a connection with these powerful people, but also talk to all of the people in the room. If you only focus on the VIPs, you might miss your next great business deal, job opportunity, or best friend. VIPs are great people to have in your network, but it's the regular people like me who will benefit you the most.

- Don't put up a fake front. Many people put up a fake front because they are afraid others won't like them if they don't. They make themselves out to be something they're not. If you own a very small company, don't tell people your company is huge! They might be impressed when you share this information, but they won't be when they find out the truth. If you drop names of powerful people, make sure you know these people. Otherwise, your reputation will suffer tremendously and others won't want to connect with you. People want to see the real you. Believe that the person you are is good enough and let your own light shine!

- Don't use an inappropriate opening line to initiate a conversation. Never start a conversation with anything too personal or controversial such as, "Hi. It's nice to meet you. What are your thoughts about abortion?," or "Hello. I'm Dave, and did you know that I used to be a woman?" These are extreme examples, but understand you need to be patient. If you put in the time, you will see great results.

- Don't use people. If you start building a reputation for using people for your own good, you will be treated as if you were a leper. If you always ask for leads and never give them out, you are using people. If you constantly ask for favors but never return them when you are asked, you are using people. If you hand out business cards to everyone only to sell your product or service, you are using people. Others were not put on this earth to help you at all times, or even most of the time. Reach out and do for others before getting anything in return. If you embrace this concept, you will never be accused of using people, and your networking will become more effective and profitable.

✔ Action Plan:

Starting today, I will do everything I can to avoid doing any of the networking no-no's.

Networking Through Golf

Play golf to level the playing field and open doors.

Q. I work for a company filled with golf fanatics. Men, women, kids—everyone loves the game. I don't play very well, but I think I should learn because I've always read golf is a great networking activity. Before I invest the money to learn to play better, can you explain why golf is such a great way to do business?

Dave: I personally think golf is the greatest game ever created, so this response might be a bit biased. But, what the heck, it's my book, and this is how I feel. Here's why:

- The pace and appeal of golf give it the upper hand over other sports. Even though football, tennis, and other sports are important entertainment venues for clients, you have limited time to socialize because of the ongoing nature of the games. With golf, you're talking and playing, not sitting in the stands watching.

- Golf levels the playing field for people in various positions at a company. While there are differences in status and power inside a company, those titles disappear on the golf course. You might be at the bottom of the company ladder, but presidents and CEOs will listen to every word that comes out of your mouth if you can help them putt better.

  A good friend of mine is a 25-year-old financial planner. His challenge is he looks much, much younger than 25. He was having trouble convincing high-worth individuals to take him seriously until he told them he was a two-handicap. For you non-golfers, that means he's really good! I recommended he talk about golf when meeting and networking with high-worth individuals, to be seen as more of an equal. Once he started using golf as a networking tool, his business took off and he's playing more golf than ever. What could be better than that?

■ Golf removes the stuffy formalities present in a business environment. Dozens of books have been written about how to address someone above you on the corporate organization chart. On the golf course, those formalities go out the window. Instead of "Nice to see you again, Ms. Johnson," or "What can I do for you today, Mr. Williamson?," it becomes, "Great shot, Jill," or "Hey Bob, what did you score on that last hole?" If you want to soften up your boss, take her out for a quick 18 holes and see what happens.

✔ Action Plan:

I will begin golfing with people I would like to create a deeper connection with by _____.

Play golf to learn about potential customers and form bonds.

Q. I understand why networking on the golf course works so well, especially when you work for a good-sized company. I own my own business and don't have a boss to shmooze. How can golf help me?

Dave: You have the opportunity to spend four hours or more with potential customers when you're on the golf course. You get to share great experiences and talk about them the next time you see them. If you accomplish anything really special while you're playing, your relationships will take a major step forward, because now your business associates and clients will talk about you and your amazing golf feat.

In December 2001, I had my first hole-in-one. It was one of the greatest experiences of my life. I can close my eyes and still see the ball drop in the hole. What's more, I now have really deep connections with the two people I was playing with because of my incredible shot. Every time I see them, it's like seeing old friends. One of the guys was a total stranger before we played.

Golf tells you so much about people. By the end of your round, you know more about these people than many of their friends do. You've had the chance to see their real personalities and their potential effects on your business relationships. If they cheat on their scorecards, there's a good chance they'll cheat or lie about their business. If they have an explosive temper on the course, you'll probably see some of that in the boardroom as well. If they continue to complain and whine three hours after a bad shot, I promise you they'll hold a grudge longer than most.

Golf-course networking can initiate a great relationship, or steer you away from a bad connection.

Off the course, if others know you golf, especially if you play well, you become a member of a powerful club. Golf is one of the most highly respected games and anyone who plays is automatically viewed in a more favorable light by other golfers. A kinship forms that doesn't exist with other kinds of activities. Some people consider those who golf to be more trustworthy and well-connected, giving people who golf a competitive advantage over those who don't. If you don't golf, this might seem a bit egotistical until you see the number of doors that golf opens. Then you will begin to understand the power of this game.

✔ Action Plan:

Starting _____, I will let more people know that I golf so I can use this wonderful game as the great networking tool it is.

Know golf networking etiquette to be successful on the course.

Q. I'm ready to grab my sticks and start networking on the golf course. I want to make the most of my time on the course. Are there any golf networking "no-no's" I should know about?

Dave: Yes. Here they are:

- Don't bring your cell phone, pager, or any other electronic device to the course. If you have to bring a cell phone, turn it off unless you need to make a call. There's nothing worse than hearing a cell phone ring when you're in the middle of a backswing or putting. Players usually get very upset over this distraction.

- Don't give golfing advice unless asked. You might think you know exactly how to fix someone's problem with his swing, grip, stance, set-up, or anything else, but most people will only get confused with additional information. If you just have to share your extensive golfing knowledge, ask permission first. Say something like, "I notice you're having a hard time putting. May I offer a few suggestions?" If he answers yes, make a few brief comments, then stop talking. This is not the time to give a lesson, and you aren't a golf pro.

- If, by some freak chance, you hit a very bad shot (which most people do, quite often), don't apologize. People who have played more than twice in their lives know even the best golfers have an occasional bad day. Just shake it off and try to do better the next time. And remember, blame only yourself. You will gain much more respect for taking total responsibility for your game.

- Conduct yourself well. Be courteous at all times. Watch the off-color jokes, and never cheat. If you smoke cigars (like I do), ask your cart partner if it's okay if you smoke. I ask everyone and no one has ever said no.

- Most importantly, never, and I mean never, try to sell your product or service on the golf course. It's not the place. It is the place to learn about people, make connections, and create friendships. You'll have plenty of time and thousands of other opportunities to close the deal.

By following these few simple rules, you'll soon learn how easy it is to make deep connections with others and, therefore, how valuable golf can be to your business.

✔ Action Plan:

Starting TODAY, I will always play golf using the highest level of etiquette possible.

Final Thoughts!!

You have just read through 49 of The Networking Guy's top 50 tips. These final two tips are the very best I can offer. Read them, and re-read them, because they can determine your networking success or failure.

50

Relax and have fun.

When you walk into a networking function, how do you normally feel? Is your stomach in knots? Are your palms sweaty? Do you wish you could stay outside? Do you feel stressed, nervous, apprehensive, or worse? If you answered yes to any of these questions, I strongly encourage you to relax and have some fun! Before you enter, take five deep breaths by inhaling through your nose and exhaling through your mouth. Remind yourself that this isn't life and death—it's just another part of doing business.

Networking is not meant to be a high-stress activity. You get to talk to potential new friends and business acquaintances. You might meet that next huge client, find your next great employee, or land that dream job. But, if after reading this book, you still really don't want to network, don't! Life is too short to do things you don't like to do.

If you enjoy networking and are ready to put forth the effort, just remember to relax, have some fun, and have faith that things will work out. You'll start to enjoy those networking functions that are now uncomfortable for you. One of my mottos is, "If it's not fun, don't do it." Make it fun, and go do it!

✔ Action Plan:

Starting today, I will make sure that I am always having fun whenever I'm networking. I will remember to relax and enjoy the chance to connect with other people.

And the Bonus Tip...

Keep a great attitude about life.

A positive attitude can lead to positive behavior and create success. An upbeat, positive person draws other people like a magnet. After all, who would you rather be around— someone who is strong and motivated, with the confidence to keep moving forward, or someone who stays stuck in one place, thinking of reasons why things don't seem to happen? It's no contest! Attitude will make everything you do work. Without it, you don't stand a chance.

You must walk into a networking session believing you will succeed. You must know, from the bottom of your heart, that you cannot fail, because if you think you might, you certainly will.

The way you think, day in and day out, affects all aspects of your life. Learn to listen to your internal dialogue. How might your thought patterns affect the way you handle stressful situations? If thoughts like, "I could never do that," or "What if I fail?," are present (like they are for most people), they can seriously impact your behavior, and in turn, every aspect of your life. If this is the case for you, you can change your internal dialogue. Try the following visualization exercise:

Visualize Success

- Picture a successful outcome to your goal or problem. What will you have, or be able to do?

- Bring this picture to mind whenever you encounter a setback, or feel concerned about your success.

Control Your Inner Voice

- If you tell yourself you cannot do something, you set yourself up for failure. Counteract negative thoughts with positive thoughts such as, "I can and will do this with a little more practice."

Reward a Job Well Done

- Reward yourself when you know you've done your best. A reward is positive reinforcement for a job well done.

- Use rewards sparingly. Save them for those times when you really deserve them.

Be a Positive Listener and Speaker

- Be positive with others and help yourself think more positively about your own challenges.

  Listen to your friends. If he or she is challenged by a project and you hear, "I can't do this," or "I will never understand," offer your friend positive reinforcement and suggestions. Tell your friend she would have a better chance of understanding the information by hiring a tutor, or setting up a strict study routine for the next week.

  Thank you to the Academic Support Center, University of Mississippi

I want you to walk in to your next networking session with the positive attitude that you can, and will, be a powerful networking professional. You will be a personal and professional resource for others and expect nothing in return. You will find out what you have to give, personally and professionally. You will overcome your fears and help other people do the same.

By maintaining this positive attitude, you will become a very powerful networking professional, your business will grow, your relationships will deepen, and your overall satisfaction with life will increase ten-fold.

Here is a poem to always remind you to keep an upbeat attitude.

> If you think you are beaten, you are.
> If you think you dare not, you don't.
> If you want to win but think you can't,
> It's almost a cinch you won't.
> If you think you'll lose, you're lost.
> For out of the world we find
> Success begins with a fellow's will.
> It's all in a state of mind.
> Life's battles don't always go
> To the stronger and faster man.
> But sooner or later the man who wins
> Is the man who thinks he can.

> —Author Unknown

✔ Action Plan:

Starting today, I will do everything I can to maintain and project a positive, outgoing attitude.

You did it!! Congratulations! You just read an insane amount of material. I included some of the greatest networking tips I know, as well as tips that others have found tremendously helpful in building their businesses and connecting more comfortably with others. You might wonder what to do now. Reading this book was the easy part. Now you need to apply what you have learned. However, a small word of caution for you. If you start using several of my tips all at the same time, there is a good chance that none of them will work for you. The way you will find the most success is by applying each one of my tips one at a time. I suggest you pick the tip that impressed you the most—the one that made you think, "What a great idea!"

Once you have selected it, start applying that tip today. Not tomorrow, or next week, or next quarter—today! Did you know that more than 85 percent of those who go through training programs or read training books never use what they've learned? Doesn't that seem like a huge waste of time? If you start using that tip today, you are automatically in the top 15 percent.

Once you have applied your first tip, select another tip and start using it that day. It doesn't matter which one you pick. What matters is that you pick one and use it. You are now in the top two percent. When was the last time you were in the top two percent of anything?

I want to thank you for reading my book. I hope you enjoyed reading it as much as I enjoyed writing it. If you have any comments, suggestions, or questions about tips I didn't cover, please e-mail me at dave@thenetworkingguy.com. Take care, and I hope your future networking is effective, comfortable, and profitable.

Are you looking for something new and exciting for your up-coming conferences, breakout sessions and corporate keynotes?

Dave Sherman, The Networking Guy™, is a nationally recognized speaker, trainer and author who has inspired thousands of people and hundreds of companies and associations how to network more effectively, more comfortably and more profitably.

Dave will challenge everything you know about networking and provide you with the tips and tools to allow you to embrace networking like you have never done before. Dave's vast business and leadership experience translates into passionate, humorous and thought-provoking presentations that will instruct you professionally, touch you personally and inspire you to network like never before.

Topics

- Seven Simple Steps of Successful Networking
- The Most Important 10 Seconds of your Career
- Fearless Networking
- Seven Simple Steps to the Perfect "Elevator Speech"
- And many more!!

Clients

- American Express
- American Marketing Association
- Association of Fundraising Professionals
- Bernard Haldane
- Child Help USA
- International Association of Financial Planners
- Medtronic
- Merrill Lynch
- National Association of Healthcare Underwriters
- National Association of Personnel Services
- National Association of Women Business Owners
- Northwestern Mutual Financial Network
- Southwest Airlines
- Wells Fargo Bank
- Over 12 different Chambers of Commerce all over the USA
- AND MANY MORE!!

Contact Information

Dave Sherman – The Networking Guy
Networking U
10128 N. 119th Place
Scottsdale, AZ 85259
480-860-6100 – Office
480-451-9484 – Fax
602-920-8700 – Mobile
Dave@thenetworkingguy.com – email
www.TheNetworkingGuy.com – Website

Give the gift of *The Networking Guy's 50 Top Tips* to your friends, family, and business associates.

❑ YES, I want _____ copies of *The Networking Guy's 50 Top Tips* at $19.95 each, plus $3.00 S&H (throughout the U. S.)

❑ YES, I want to receive my FREE subscription to *Networking Central* e-zine.
My email address is listed below.

❑ YES, I am interested in having The Networking Guy™ speak to my organization. Please contact me with details.

My check or money order for $ _____ is enclosed.
Please make your check payable to The Networking Guy, LLC

Please charge my:
❑ Visa ❑ MasterCard ❑ American Express
Credit card # _____

Expiration date (month/year)_____/_____
Name_____
Organization_____
Address _____
City_____State _____Zip_____
Phone_____Fax_____
Email (please print clearly)_____

Signature X_____

Return to:
The Networking Guy, LLC
10128 N. 119th Place
Scottsdale, AZ 85259
Telephone Orders: 480-860-6100
Fax Orders: 480-451-9484
Internet Orders: www.thenetworkingguy.com